# FRANCHISING IN DEMOCRATIC REPUBLIC OF THE CONGO 2014

*Legal and Business Considerations*

KENDAL H. TYRE, JR., EXECUTIVE EDITOR
DIANA VILMENAY-HAMMOND, MANAGING EDITOR
COURTNEY L. LINDSAY, II, ASSISTANT EDITOR

LEXNOIR FOUNDATION

FIRST QUARTER 2014

LexNoir Foundation is the charitable, educational arm of LexNoir, an international network of lawyers connecting the African Diaspora.

This publication, *Franchising in Democratic Republic of the Congo 2014: Legal and Business Considerations*, contains excerpts from *Franchising in Africa 2014: Legal and Business Considerations*. Both works are published by LexNoir Foundation and reflect the points of view of the authors and editors as of the date of publication and do not necessarily represent the opinions, interpretations, or positions of the law firms or organizations with which they are affiliated, nor the opinions, interpretations or positions of LexNoir Foundation or LexNoir.

Nothing contained in this book is to be considered as the rendering of legal advice, either generally or in connection with any specific issues or case. Readers are responsible for obtaining advice from their own legal counsel or other professional. This book, any forms and agreements or other information herein are intended for educational and informational purposes only.

www.lexnoir.org

# Table of Contents

## *Franchising in Democratic Republic of the Congo*

Emery Mukendi Wafwana, Nady Mayifuila Dina, Jonathan van Kempen, Edouard Laddy Tshishimbi Mpamba, Emmanuel Otshudiema Bengu and Dr. Sancy Lenoble Matschinga
Emery Mukendi Wafwana & Associates

# Bibliography of International Franchise Resources

Kendal H. Tyre, Jr., Diana Vilmenay-Hammond, Pierce Haesung Han, Courtney L. Lindsay, II and Keri McWilliams
Nixon Peabody LLP

# Acknowledgment

This book could not have been written without the hard work and dedication of each of the contributing authors and editors. Thank you.

We would like to acknowledge and extend our heartfelt gratitude to Michael Collier and Maria Stallings of the Washington, D.C. office of Nixon Peabody LLP for their invaluable assistance in revising, proofing, and editing this publication.

# About the Editors and Authors

**Kendal H. Tyre, Jr.** – Kendal is a partner in the Washington, D.C. office of Nixon Peabody LLP. He handles domestic and cross-border transactions, including mergers and acquisitions, joint ventures, strategic alliances, licensing, and franchise matters.

In his franchise and licensing practice, Kendal counsels domestic and international franchisors, franchisees, licensors, licensees and distributors regarding U.S. state and federal franchise laws as well as foreign franchise legislation in a variety of jurisdictions. Kendal drafts and provides advice with regard to franchise and license agreements, disclosure documents and area development agreements and has extensive experience drafting and negotiating a variety of other commercial agreements. His client base spans the United States and foreign countries, including South Africa, Kenya, and the United Kingdom.

Kendal is a frequent contributor to franchise publications and a frequent speaker at franchise programs held by the American Bar Association Forum on Franchising and the International Franchise Association.

Kendal is co-chair of the firm's Diversity Action Committee and its Africa Group. Kendal is also the executive director of LexNoir Foundation.

E-mail address: ktyre@nixonpeabody.com

**Diana Vilmenay-Hammond** – Diana is an attorney in the Washington, D.C. office of Nixon Peabody LLP. She is a member of the firm's Franchise & Distribution Team.

In her franchise practice, Diana works with domestic and international franchisors on transactional and litigation matters. Specifically, she counsels franchisor clients regarding state and federal franchise laws, disclosure and registration obligations.

Diana drafts and negotiates various commercial agreements, including international franchise and development agreements.

Diana has co-authored numerous articles on franchising and frequently co-hosted the Nixon Peabody franchise law webinar series. Topics have included:

- "Franchise Case Law Round-Up: Implications for Your Franchise," February 15, 2012;
- "Social Media Part II: Best Practices in Protecting Your Brand in the New Media," September 14, 2010; and
- "The Awuah Case: Bellwether or Outlier," May 11, 2010

Diana received her J.D. from Howard University School of Law and her B.A. from Georgetown University. She is a member of the American Bar Association (Forum on Franchising).

Email address: dvilmenay@nixonpeabody.com

**Pierce Haesung Han** – Pierce is an associate in Nixon Peabody's Global Business & Transactions Group. Pierce focuses his practice on three main areas, assisting clients with a variety of complex business transactions.

- Mergers & Acquisitions: Providing assistance to both public and private clients with various mergers and acquisitions, performing due diligence, drafting and negotiating transaction documents, and facilitating closing and post-closing mechanics.
- International Commercial Transactions: Drafting and negotiating a variety of commercial agreements, including international franchise and development agreements, license agreements, and purchase and sale agreements.
- Federal Securities Law Matters: Assisting public and private clients regarding federal securities laws and stock exchange rules relating to corporate governance and disclosure.

Pierce serves as the Secretary of the Asian Pacific Bar Association Educational Fund (an affiliate of the Asian Pacific American Bar Association of the Greater Washington, D.C. Area).

Pierce received his J.D. from Georgetown University Law Center and his B.A. from Case Western Reserve University. He is admitted to practice in the State of New York and the District of Columbia.

E-mail address: phan@nixonpeabody.com

**Courtney L. Lindsay, II** – Courtney is an associate in Nixon Peabody's Corporate and Finance practice. In his corporate practice, Courtney assists for-profit and non-profit entities with transactional matters and corporate governance. In various capacities, Courtney has been involved in multiple merger and acquisition transactions, including drafting and managing due diligence.

Previously, Courtney worked in the legal and business affairs department at a national cable network, where he handled matters related to the network's LLC agreement, including drafting board and member consent agreements.

Courtney received his J.D. from the University of Virginia School of Law and his B.A. from the University of Virginia. He is admitted to practice in the Commonwealth of Virginia and the District of Columbia.

E-mail address: clindsay@nixonpeabody.com

**Keri McWilliams** – Keri is an associate in the Franchise & Distribution team of Nixon Peabody LLP. Keri works with clients on a number of franchising issues, including obtaining and maintaining franchise registrations in various states, responding to state inquiries regarding trade practices, ongoing compliance with state and federal regulations, and updating franchise disclosure documents. She also handles franchise sales counseling and franchise system issues.

# Franchising in Democratic Republic of the Congo

*Emery Mukendi Wafwana, Nady Mayifuila Dina,
Jonathan van Kempen, Edouard Laddy Tshishimbi
Mpamba, Emmanuel Otshudiema Bengu and Dr.
Sancy Lenoble Matschinga*

*Emery Mukendi Wafwana & Associates*

**Kinshasa/Gombe, DRC**

# Democratic Republic of the Congo

Under the DRC law there are no restrictions on a franchisor to restrict transfers by a master franchisee, any interest in a master franchisee, or the assets of the master franchisee; or on the ability of a master franchisee to control and/or restrict transfers of a subfranchisee's rights under a master franchise agreement, interest in the subfranchisee, or the assets of the subfranchisee.

Since franchising is generally regulated by contract law, most of the obligations of the parties are usually governed by the terms of the parties' agreement, thus everything depends on the will of the respective parties. The parties may agree on any provision that is not against the law or public policy.

## VII. Termination

*Please advise us as to any laws relating to termination in your country, such as agency laws, required indemnity provisions, notice or "good cause" requirements, or other laws affecting termination of a franchise agreement. Please describe.*

In the DRC, there is currently no specific law on agency or distributorship agreements. Agreements such as franchise agreements are governed by general contract law rules set in the DRC *Civil Law Code*. According to Article 33 of the *Civil Law Code*, terms and conditions set in contracts form the law between the parties. It is, however, worth mentioning that commercial leases and their termination clauses are regulated by specific laws. Notice to terminate a commercial lease is six months. Notice for termination of an employment contract is also regulated in the DRC. Congolese labor law provides that duration of notice is increased with seven working days for each full year of continuous employment.

Franchise agreement may also be terminated due to an unforeseen occurrence or good cause.

# Democratic Republic of the Congo

## VIII. Governing Law, Jurisdiction, and Dispute Resolution

### A. Choice of Law of Foreign Jurisdiction

*Please confirm whether the choice of law of a foreign jurisdiction would likely to be upheld under the law of the country, except for certain matters such as trademarks, bankruptcy, and competition matters, which we assume would be governed by the law in your country.*

The choice of law of a foreign jurisdiction would be upheld under the law of the DRC. The DRC judges will, in principle, enforce franchise agreements governed by foreign law, subject to their compliance with mandatory or public order rules. Matters relating to real estate law, incorporation of companies and creation of security interests, tax and customs law, trademarks, bankruptcy and labor law will necessarily be subject to the DRC law.

### B. International Arbitration Dispute Resolution

*Please confirm that a court in your country would honor an election of international arbitration dispute resolution, and therefore refuse to hear any disputes arising under a franchise agreement.*

The choice of an international arbitration dispute resolution clause by the parties is authorized by the DRC law as long as the parties agreed upon it. Currently, foreign arbitral awards rendered outside of OHADA member states are recognized and enforced in the DRC after a tribunal of competent authority has rendered an enforcement decision.

Nevertheless, this situation will soon change because a law authorizing the ratification of the New York Convention was recently promulgated. The New York Convention will enter into force in the DRC on the ninety day following the date of deposit by the DRC of its instrument of ratification or accession. It should be noted, however, that the DRC made four reservations to the New York Convention.[4] Foreign arbitral awards rendered in other OHADA member states are recognized and enforced in the DRC according to the rules established in the OHADA Uniform Act on Arbitration.

## IX.    Non-Competition Provisions

*If the franchise agreement prohibits the master franchisee from engaging in certain competitive activities during the term of the agreement, and for a 12-month period after the termination or expiration of the agreement, please comment on the enforceability of non-competition covenants in your country.*

As previously stated, since franchise is a non-regulated agreement, parties are free to agree on the existence of a non-competition provision and its terms, but always in compliance with general principles of the law.

Non-competition clauses are common in practice. Some guidance may be found in labor law where non-competition clauses are regulated. When such clauses are permissible, they may not exceed one year after the termination of the employment contract and their scope must be limited to the activities covered under the employment contract.

Furthermore, the Industrial Property Law provides that clauses contained in the licensing contracts relating to these contracts

---

[4]    A first reservation, based on the principle of reciprocity, provides that arbitral awards made in the territory of states that have not ratified or acceded to the convention are not eligible for the enforcement of arbitral awards on DRC territory. A second reservation provides that only awards on matters considered "commercial" under national law will be recognized and enforced in the DRC. A third reservation notes that only arbitral awards made after the accession of the DRC to the New York Convention may be enforced under it. This reservation confirms the principle of non-retroactivity. Finally, the last reservation provides that the New York Convention does not apply to disputes related to real estate property located in the considered state or on a right related to such property.

Christopher A. Nowak, John Pratt, and Carl E. Zwisler, *Franchising Internationally with Countries with Opaque Legal Systems* W20, ABA FORUM ON FRANCHISING (2006)

E. Lynn Perry and John L. Sullivan Jr., *Trademark Compliance and Enforcement Techniques* E/W12, ABA FORUM ON FRANCHISING (1992)

Marcel Portmann, *Franchising Sector Proves Global Reach*, in FRANCHISING WORLD (January 2007)

John Pratt and Luiz Henrique O. do Amaral, *Civil Law for Common Law Practitioners (or How to Draft an Agreement for Use Overseas)* W4, ABA FORUM ON FRANCHISING (2002)

Kirk W. Reilly, Robert F. Salkowski and Geoffrey B. Shaw, *Determining the Rules of Engagement in Litigation Here and Abroad* W5, ABA FORUM ON FRANCHISING (2008)

Catherine Riesterer and Frank Zaid, *Basics of International Franchising* L/B2, ABA FORUM ON FRANCHISING (1997)

W. Andrew Scott and Christopher N. Wormald, *Stranger in a Strange Land: Contrasting Franchising in International Expansion* W2, ABA FORUM ON FRANCHISING (2003)

Donald Smith and Erik Wulff, *International Franchising: The Unraveling of an International Franchise Relationship* 15/W13, ABA FORUM ON FRANCHISING (1993)

Frank Zaid, Pamela Mills, and Michael Santa Maria, *Essential Issues in International Franchising* LB/1, ABA FORUM ON FRANCHISING (2001)

## II. African Resources

Joyce G. Mazero and J. Perry Maisonneuve, *Franchising in the Middle East and North Africa* W2, ABA FORUM ON FRANCHISING (2009)

Kendal H. Tyre, Jr. and Diana Vilmenay-Hammond, *Franchise World: A Burgeoning Middle Class Spurs Franchise Investment in Africa*, MINORITY BUSINESS ENTREPRENEUR (November 2012)

Kendal H. Tyre, Jr., *IP Protection May Promote Additional Franchise Growth in Africa*, NIXON PEABODY LLP: FRANCHISING BUSINESS & LAW ALERT (September 2012)

Kendal H. Tyre, Jr., *Market Potential for Franchising in Africa*, NIXON PEABODY LLP: FRANCHISING BUSINESS & LAW ALERT (June 2011)

Kendal H. Tyre, Jr. and Courtney L. Lindsay, II, *Continued Growth of Franchising in Africa*, NIXON PEABODY LLP: FRANCHISE LAW ALERT (April 2013)

Kendal H. Tyre, Jr. and Courtney L. Lindsay, II, *Pan African Franchise Federation Holds Inaugural Meeting*, NIXON PEABODY LLP: AFRICA ALERT (June 2013)

Kendal H. Tyre, Jr. and Courtney L. Lindsay, II, *White House Encouraging Private Investment and Transparency in Sub-Saharan Africa*, NIXON PEABODY LLP: AFRICA ALERT (August 2012)

Kendal H. Tyre, Jr. and Diana Vilmenay-Hammond, *African Economic Growth Impacts Franchising on the Continent*, NIXON PEABODY LLP: FRANCHISE LAW ALERT (July 2012)

Kendal H. Tyre, Jr. and Diana Vilmenay-Hammond, *Franchising in Africa*, in FRANCHISING WORLD (August 2013)

John Sotos and Sam Hall, *African Franchising: Cross-Continent Momentum*, in FRANCHISING WORLD (June 2007)

## A.    Angola

João Afonso Fialho, *Franchising in Angola*, in FRANCHISING IN AFRICA: LEGAL AND BUSINESS CONSIDERATIONS 91-105 (Kendal H. Tyre, Jr. & Diana Vilmenay-Hammond eds. 2012)

## B.    Botswana

Bonzo Makgalemele, *Franchising in Botswana*, in FRANCHISING IN AFRICA: LEGAL AND BUSINESS CONSIDERATIONS 107-117 (Kendal H. Tyre, Jr. & Diana Vilmenay-Hammond eds. 2012)

## C.    Cape Verde

João Afonso Fialho, *Franchising in Cape Verde*, in FRANCHISING IN AFRICA: LEGAL AND BUSINESS CONSIDERATIONS 119-132 (Kendal H. Tyre, Jr. & Diana Vilmenay-Hammond eds. 2012)

## D.    Egypt

Girgis Abd El-Shahid, *Franchising in Eqypt*, in FRANCHISING IN AFRICA: LEGAL AND BUSINESS CONSIDERATIONS 133-142 (Kendal H. Tyre, Jr. & Diana Vilmenay-Hammond eds. 2012)

A. Safaa El Din El Oteifi, *Egypt*, in INTERNATIONAL FRANCHISING EGY/1 (Dennis Campbell gen. ed. 2011)

## E.    Ethiopia

Yohannes Assefa and Biset Beyene Molla, *Franchising in Ethiopia*, in FRANCHISING IN AFRICA: LEGAL AND BUSINESS CONSIDERATIONS 143-157 (Kendal H. Tyre, Jr. & Diana Vilmenay-Hammond eds. 2012)

Kendal H. Tyre, Jr., Yohannes Assefa and Getachew Mengistie Alemu, *New Intellectual Property Regulation Requires Scramble to Protect Marks in Ethiopia*, NIXON PEABODY LLP: AFRICA ALERT (October 2013)

## F.    Ghana

Divine K.D. Letsa and Hawa Tejansie Ajei, *Franchising in Ghana*, in FRANCHISING IN AFRICA: LEGAL AND BUSINESS CONSIDERATIONS 159-167 (Kendal H. Tyre, Jr. & Diana Vilmenay-Hammond eds. 2012)

Keri is a member of the American Bar Association's Forum on Franchising, and the Federal and Minnesota State bar associations. She is also a member of Minnesota Women Lawyers and the Minnesota Association of Black Lawyers, and a volunteer in the Volunteer Lawyers Network.

Keri received her J.D. from the Georgetown University Law Center and her B.F.A. from Washington University. She is admitted to practice in the District of Columbia and Minnesota.

E-mail address: kmcwilliams@nixonpeabody.com

**Emery Mukendi Wafwana** – Emery is the Founding Partner of Emery Mukendi Wafwana & Associés, created in 1995. His areas of practice include mining and hydrocarbon law, electrical power law, energy law, investment law, corporate law, aviation law, OHADA law, intellectual property law, legal evaluation of projects and litigation. Emery was awarded by the "International Who's Who Legal Of Mining Lawyers 2012" as a legal expert in mining law. He is also founder and Chief Editor of Juricongo, a legal website and portal of Congolese Law (www.juricongo.com). Emery holds his law degree in economic and social law from the University of Kinshasa. He speaks French, English, Lingala and Tshiluba.

E-mail address: ewafwana@cabemery.org

**Nady Mayifuila Dina** – Nady is an associate and office manager of the New York branch of Emery Mukendi Wafwana & Associés. She joined the firm in 2010. Her practice includes business law (USA, DRC & OHADA), mining, energy and natural resources (DRC & OHADA), corporate law (USA, DRC & OHADA), foreign direct investment in French-speaking Africa as well as U.S. federal and state litigation. She holds a JD in private law and civil procedure and a JD in business law. She also holds a Master's Degree in European business law and a LL.M. degree in banking, corporate and finance laws from Fordham University, School of Law. She speaks French, English, Italian and Lingala.

E-mail address: mayifuila@cabemery.org

**Jonathan van Kempen** – Admitted to the New York Bar (2012) and Bar of Brussels (2005). Mr. Jonathan van Kempen is an associate and joined the law firm Emery Mukendi Wafwana & Associates in 2012. His areas of practice include corporate law, mining and hydrocarbon law, international mergers and acquisitions, OHADA law, international contracts and project finance in natural resources, energy and infrastructures in Africa, particularly in Francophone Africa. Mr. Jonathan van Kempen holds his law degree from the Catholic University of Louvain (Belgium) since 2002. He holds a master degree in German and international law from the Georg-August University of Göttingen (Germany) and a post-graduate in business management from the HUB of Brussels (Belgium). He also holds a LL.M. in international business and trade law from Fordham University, School of Law (New York). He speaks French, English, German and Dutch.

E-mail address: vankempen@cabemery.org

**Edouard Laddy Tshishimbi Mpamba** – Edouard has been an associate of Emery Mukendi Wafwana & Associés since 2013. His areas of practice include business and corporate, hydrocarbon, public procurement, mining, investment, land and real estate, intellectual property law and litigation. Edouard received his law degree in private law from the University of Lubumbashi in 2002. He also has a background in international criminal law having worked as law clerk at the office of the prosecutor of the International Criminal Court at the Hague. He speaks English, French, Tshiluba, Lingala and Swahili.

E-mail address: ltmpamba@cabemery.org

**Emmanuel Otshudiema Bengu** – Emmanuel has been an associate at Emery Mukendi Wafwana & Associés since 2009. His areas of practice include contract, land and real estate, corporate, general commercial, labor and social security, mining, hydrocarbon, and OHADA law. Emmanuel received his law degree in economic and social law from the University of

Kinshasa in 2006. He speaks French, Lingala, Tshiluba, Otetela and Swahili.

E-mail address: otshudiema@cabemery.org

**Dr. Sancy Lenoble Matschinga** – Sancy is a Juriste International of Emery Mukendi Wafwana & Associés. Prior to joining the law firm in 2013, he worked in several law firms in France, in the French Ministry of Interior (Department of Homeland Security), and the French Council of State. His areas of practice include public business law (public contracts, European public procurement, infrastructures, public-private partnerships). His areas of practice also include mining and hydrocarbon, and natural resources and investment law in French-speaking African countries. Sancy holds a Ph.D. in public law, a Post-Master's degree in public and private law of economics from Evry Val d'Essonne University, a Master's degree in public business law from Paris 1 Panthéon-Sorbonne University, and a Master's degree in law from Marien-Ngouabi University. He also holds the bar certification of attorney-at-law from Paris Bar School. In 2012, he was certified with a Master Series for Distinguished Leaders from Skinner Leadership Institute in Washington, D.C. He is a member of the French-American Bar Association and he speaks French, English, Lingala and Munukutuba.

E-mail address: smatschinga@cabemery.org

# About the Book

*Franchising in Democratic Republic of the Congo 2014: Legal and Business Considerations* contains excerpts from the larger work, *Franchising in Africa 2014: Legal and Business Considerations.* Both books serve as practical, succinct, easy-to-use reference tools for lawyers, business people and academics to use in navigating the myriad laws and business issues impacting franchise arrangements on the African continent.

This book provides an overview of the franchise industry in Democratic Republic of the Congo and addresses the typical legal issues confronted when expanding a franchise system in Democratic Republic of the Congo. The larger work, *Franchising in Africa 2014: Legal and Business Considerations*, covers those laws governing franchising in fifteen other African countries – Angola, Botswana, Burundi, Cape Verde, Egypt, Ethiopia, Ghana, Kenya, Mozambique, Nigeria, Rwanda, South Africa, Tunisia, Zambia and Zimbabwe.

In both books, an author, who is a legal expert in the designated jurisdiction, addresses the basic questions that a franchise lawyer would need to know to competently represent a client in expanding their franchise system to that country.

Each country chapter organizes a discussion of that country's laws under various headings and in a uniform format. Topics were sent to each country's author in the form of a questionnaire, and each author drafted responses to the questions presented. A general overview relating to the political and economic history of the country at the beginning of each chapter provides an initial context for the regulatory framework.[1]

---

[1]   The source of information for these sections is the Central Intelligence Agency, https://www.cia.gov/library/publications/the-world-factbook/ (last visited November 3, 2013).

Apart from an overview of the legal framework for franchising, each book contains other articles and resources that should prove useful to those in the franchise industry.

The authors for each chapter are listed at the beginning of a chapter and their biographical information is listed in the previous section, *About the Editors and Authors*.

Readers should always consult with local counsel in the relevant jurisdiction instead of relying solely on the information contained in this book. The laws governing franchising are evolving and local counsel in Democratic Republic of the Congo are best positioned to provide timely, relevant advice applying the current law to the particular facts of a case.

# Democratic Republic of the Congo

## I.    Introduction

### A.    Historical Background of Country

The Democratic Republic of the Congo ("DRC"), formerly known as Zaire, is located in central Africa, surrounded by nine neighboring countries.

The DRC is a civil law country, whose private law is based on the *1804 Napoleonic Civil Code*. The general characteristics of the DRC legal system are very similar to legal systems in force in other French-speaking African countries. At the apex of the legal system, the *DRC Constitution of February 18, 2006* is the first source of law.

Since September 12, 2012, all provisions of the *Organization for Business Law in Africa* ("OHADA") Treaty[2] as well as *OHADA Uniform Acts* are applicable in the DRC.[3] This set of applicable laws brings increased modernity and reliability to the domestic legal system, as well as a new court, the Common Court of Justice and Arbitration ("CCJA"). It is the highest competent court in the DRC for matters covered by the OHADA Uniform Acts.

Various legal areas not covered by the *OHADA Uniform Acts* are also being reformed. For example, reforms in the insurance and electricity sectors are planned to end the State's monopoly in these sectors. The DRC, notably through the creation of the national agency for the investment promotion (*Agence Nationale pour la Promotion de l'Investissement* "ANAPI") and the steering committee for the improvement of the business and

---

[2]    OHADA is an African organization, establish on October 17, 1993, which currently counts 17 member states, including Benin, Burkina Faso, Cameroon, Central African Republic, Chad, the Republic of Congo, Comoros, Cote d'Ivoire, the DRC, Equatorial Guinea, Gabon, Guinea, Guinea Bissau, Mali, Niger, Senegal and Togo.

[3]    There are currently nine uniform acts promulgated by OHADA, including a uniform act on commercial law and a uniform act on agreements of transportation of goods by road.

investment climate (*Comité de Pilotage pour l'Amélioration du Climat des Affaires et des Investissements* "CPCAI") as well as its legal reforms, has shown a willingness to facilitate and increase investments. Such a desire is confirmed by the DRC's imminent accession to the *New York Convention on the Recognition and Enforcement of Foreign Arbitral Awards* of June 10, 1958 (the "New York Convention").

## B.    Economy of the Country

The DRC is immensely rich in natural resources and holds some of the world's largest mineral deposits, which play an important role in the DRC economy. DRC's economy grew 7.2% in 2012 and as agriculture and extractive industries remain pillars of the DRC economy, increasing global demands in minerals and investments in the sector should keep the economy growing. The mining industry contributes about 28% to the country's GDP.

## C.    Franchise Legal Overview

Under DRC law, there is no specific law that regulates franchise agreements and/or transactions. The franchise agreement is seen as a contractual agreement between parties and thus contract law will govern such an agreement.

However, specific laws or regulations governing certain areas, such as labor law or laws regulating commercial leases may have an impact on a particular franchise agreement.

# II.    Regulatory Requirements

## A.    Pre-Sale Disclosure

*Please describe any pre-sale franchise disclosure or similar requirements that may apply to franchise transactions.*

No pre-sale franchise disclosure or similar requirements apply to franchise transactions under the DRC law.

# Democratic Republic of the Congo

### B.     Governmental Approvals, Registrations, Filing Requirements

*Please describe any necessary government approvals, registrations, or filing requirements that may apply to franchise transactions.*

There is no specific requirement under the DRC law for government approvals, registrations, or filing requirements for franchise transactions. However, see Section V of this chapter on trademark licenses regulated under *Law n°82-001 of January 7, 1982 on Industrial Property* (the "Industrial Property Law").

### C.     Limits of Fees and Typical Term of Franchise Agreement

*Please describe any limits upon the nature and extent of fees and the term of a typical franchise agreement.*

As stated, a franchise agreement is a contractual agreement between parties. According to the DRC law, parties are free to enter into any contractual agreement, to agree on any terms and conditions and to be bound by the terms to which they agree. There are no specific guidelines on term limits applicable to franchise agreements; therefore, parties are free to indicate the duration of the agreement. Nevertheless, the agreement must not be contrary to mandatory rules and/or DRC public policy law.

## III.  Currency

*If all payments under a franchise agreement must be made in immediately available U.S. Dollars, please advise as to any restrictions, reporting requirements, or regulations concerning the exchange, repatriation, or remittance of U.S. Dollars.*

There are no specific restrictions on parties transacting in U.S. Dollars. All repatriation or remittance must be made through an approved DRC bank. The following fees and restrictions apply to remittances. First, the Central Bank of Congo ("BCC") levies a change royalty of 2% on any payment to or from a foreign country regardless of the status of the transferor or transferee; second, cross-border transfers to and from the DRC, with a value equal to or greater than US$ 10,000 must be made through an approved credit institution or intermediary and has to be made on a specific form, known as RC declaration; third, revenues (remuneration, income, dividends, leasehold, interests, etc.) can only be received or transferred through an approved DRC bank.

Repayments of loans, principal and interests are made in accordance with the terms of the agreement, and require the use of a RC declaration to be issued by a DRC approved bank.

There is generally no obligation to repatriate foreign earnings to the DRC, except amounts received in payment for the export of goods or services. These must be repatriated through an approved bank within the time frame specified in the BCC's exchange regulations.

## IV.    Taxes, Tariffs, and Duties

*Please do not provide any in-depth comments on tax structuring. However, please provide your general comments on the typical amount of withholding tax that would apply and whether a "gross-up" provision contained in a franchise agreement would be enforceable in your country.*

The DRC general tax system provides for direct and indirect taxes. Direct taxes are subdivided between asset-based taxes, which include taxes on real property and on vehicles, and income based taxes, which include taxes on rental income, taxes on interests and dividends, and professional taxes, which comprise taxes on profits and taxes on salaries. Indirect taxes include Value Added Tax ("VAT"). The DRC tax system provides for a withholding obligation for dividends and interests which are annually taxed at the rate of 22%. Net profits made through activities undertaken in the DRC are taxed at the rate of 40%. The DRC tax system also provides for VAT payable on the gross amount of sales of products or services. Standard VAT rate is 16%.

The DRC entered into a double tax treaty with Belgium, which came into force on December 24, 2011, and with South Africa, which came into force on July 18, 2012.

Gross-up provisions may be permissible depending on the agreement made between the parties to a contractual agreement.

## V.    Trademarks

*Please advise us as to whether there are any special requirements for granting a valid trademark license, including the use of a registered user agreement or a short trademark license agreement and any required filing of such an agreement with the trademark authorities.*

In the DRC, industrial and intellectual properties are primarily governed by the Industrial Property Law and *Ordinance-law n°86-033 of April 5, 1986 on the Protection of Copyrights and Neighboring Rights.*

Owners of trademark rights are entitled to enter into license agreements to license the use of trademarks to other parties. A Trademark license agreement needs to be in writing and an original of the license trademark must be filed and registered with the Ministry of Intellectual Property along with registration fees.

## VI.    Restrictions on Transfer

*Please advise as to whether there are any restrictions (1) on a franchisor to restrict transfers by a master franchisee, any interest in a master franchisee, or the assets of the master franchisee or (2) the ability of a master franchisee to control and/or restrict transfers of a subfranchisee's rights under a master franchise agreement, interest in the subfranchisee, or the assets of the subfranchisee.*

shall be null and void if they impose limitations on the licensee, which do not arise from the rights conferred by the license. Nevertheless, the following shall not be considered unlawful limitations: (i) limitations concerning the measurement, scope, quantity, territory or term of the exploitation of the subject of the license (ii) limitations imposed by the licensor to ensure the best possible technical working of the license; (iii) the obligation imposed upon the licensee to refrain from any act likely to infringe the rights of the licensor.

Therefore, non-competition clause shall be, in principle, acceptable under the Industrial Property Law, provided that they are not in contrary with mandatory rules or public policy rules.

## X.    Language Requirements

*Does the law in your country require that a franchise agreement be translated into the local language in order to be enforceable between the parties?*

The DRC law does not require that a franchise agreement be translated into the local language to be enforceable between the parties. However, it must be translated into French, which is the DRC official language, if the franchise agreement is presented to DRC courts or administration.

## XI.    Other Significant Matters

*Please advise as to whether there are any significant matters not addressed above of which a franchisor should be aware in connection with its entering into a franchise agreement in your country.*

There are no other significant matters to be addressed.

# Democratic Republic of the Congo

# Bibliography of International Franchise Resources

*Kendal H. Tyre, Jr., Diana Vilmenay-Hammond, Pierce Haesung Han, Courtney L. Lindsay, II and Keri McWilliams*

*Nixon Peabody LLP*

**Washington, D.C.**

## I.    General International Resources

Mark Abell, Gary R. Duvall, and Andrea Oricchio Kirsh, *International Franchise Legislation* B1, ABA FORUM ON FRANCHISING (1996)

Kathleen C. Anderson and Anthony M. Stiegler, *Put Muscle in Your Marks: Enforcing Intellectual Property Rights* W14, ABA FORUM ON FRANCHISING (1995)

Richard M. Asbill and Jane W. LaFranchi, *International Franchise Sales Laws—A Survey* W7, ABA FORUM ON FRANCHISING (2005)

Jeffery A. Brimer, Alison C. McElroy, and John Pratt, *Going International: What Additional Restraints Will You Face?* W4, ABA FORUM ON FRANCHISING (2011)

Michael G. Brennan, Alexander Konigsberg, and Philip F. Zeidman, *Globetrotting: A Workshop on International Franchising* 10/W8, ABA FORUM ON FRANCHISING (1994)

Michael G. Brennan, Alexander Konigsberg, and Philip F. Zeidman, *Globetrotting: Strategies for Launching U.S. Franchisors Abroad* 2/P2, ABA FORUM ON FRANCHISING (1994)

Christopher P. Bussert and Jennifer Dolman, *Regaining Your Trademark After Abandonment or Misappropriation* W7, ABA FORUM ON FRANCHISING (2011)

Ronald T. Coleman and Linda K. Stevens, *Trade Secrets and Confidential Information: Rights and Remedies* W2, ABA FORUM ON FRANCHISING (2000)

Finola Cunningham, *Commerce Department Helps Franchisors Go Global*, in FRANCHISING WORLD 63 (Dec. 2005)

Michael R. Daigle and Alex S. Konigsberg, *Meeting Off-Shore Disclosure and Contract Requirements* F/W13, ABA FORUM ON FRANCHISING (1992)

Jennifer Dolman, Robert A. Lauer, and Lawrence M. Weinberg, *Structuring International Master Franchise Relationships for Success and Responding When Things Go Awry* W22, ABA FORUM ON FRANCHISING (2007)

Gary R. Duvall, Paul Jones, and Jane LaFranchi, *Planning for the International Enforcement of Franchise Agreements* W6, ABA FORUM ON FRANCHISING (1999)

William Edwards, *International Expansion: Do Opportunities Outweigh Challenges?* in FRANCHISING WORLD (February 2008)

George J. Eydt and Stuart Hershman, *Bringing a Foreign Franchise System to the United States* W9, ABA FORUM ON FRANCHISING (2009)

William A. Finkelstein and Louis T. Pirkey, *International Trademarks* W15, ABA FORUM ON FRANCHISING (1991)

William A. Finkelstein, *Protecting Trademarks Internationally: Current Strategies and Developments* B3, ABA FORUM ON FRANCHISING (1996)

Stephen Giles, Lou H. Jones, and Lawrence Weinberg, *Negotiating and Documenting Complex International Franchise Agreements* W21, ABA FORUM ON FRANCHISING (2006)

Steven M. Goldman, Stephen Giles, Marc Israel, and Stanley Wong, *Competition Round Up from Around the World* LB2, ABA FORUM ON FRANCHISING (2004)

David C. Gryce and E. Lynn Perry, *Trademarks and Copyrights in the International Arena* 6/W4, ABA FORUM ON FRANCHISING (1993)

Kenneth S. Kaplan, Andrew P. Loewinger, and Penelope J. Ward, *System Standards in International Franchising* W14, ABA FORUM ON FRANCHISING (2005)

Edward Levitt and Jorge Mondragon, *A Survey of International Legal Traps and How to Avoid Them—Beyond the Franchise Laws* W20, ABA FORUM ON FRANCHISING (2007)

Ned Levitt, Kendal H. Tyre, and Penny Ward, *The Impossible Dream: Controlling Your International Franchise System* W4, ABA FORUM ON FRANCHISING (2010)

Michael K. Lindsey and Andrew P. Loewinger, *International (Non-U.S.) Franchise Disclosure Requirements* W9, ABA FORUM ON FRANCHISING (2002)

Andrew P. Loewinger and John Pratt, *Recent Changes and Trends in International Franchise Laws* W4, ABA FORUM ON FRANCHISING (2008)

Andrew P. Loewinger and Thomas M. Pitegoff, *Avoiding the Long Arm of the Law in International Franchising: Issues and Approaches* W8, ABA FORUM ON FRANCHISING (1995)

Craig J. Madson and Katherine C. Spelman, *Similarity and Confusion in the Intellectual Property Arena* W11, ABA FORUM ON FRANCHISING (1997)

## G.   Libya

Kendal H. Tyre, Jr. & Diana Vilmenay-Hammond, *First U.S. Franchise Opens in Libya*, NIXON PEABODY LLP: AFRICA ALERT (August 2012)

## H.   Mozambique

Diogo Xavier da Cunha, *Franchising in Mozambique*, in FRANCHISING IN AFRICA: LEGAL AND BUSINESS CONSIDERATIONS 169-182 (Kendal H. Tyre, Jr. & Diana Vilmenay-Hammond eds. 2012)

## I.   Nigeria

Theo Emuwa and Bimbola Fowler-Ekar, *Franchising in Nigeria*, in FRANCHISING IN AFRICA: LEGAL AND BUSINESS CONSIDERATIONS 183-198 (Kendal H. Tyre, Jr. & Diana Vilmenay-Hammond eds. 2012)

Kendal H. Tyre, Jr. and Theo Emuwa, *Nigerian Franchising: Making Your Way Through the Thicket*, NIXON PEABODY LLP: FRANCHISE LAW ALERT (June 2005)

## J.   South Africa

Eugene Honey, *Franchising and the New Consumer Protection Bill*, BOWMAN GILFILLAN (March 2008)

Eugene Honey, *Franchising and the Consumer Protection Bill*, BOWMAN GILFILLAN (May 2008)

Eugene Honey, *Pitfalls and Difficulties with the CPA*, ADAMS & ADAMS (March 2013)

Eugene Honey, *Disclosure is Compulsory*, ADAMS & ADAMS (May 2013)

Eugene Honey and Wim Alberts, *Fundamental Consumer Rights: The Right to Equality*, BOWMAN GILFILLAN (March 2009)

Eugene Honey and Wim Alberts, *The Reach of the Consumer Protection Bill: The Final*, BOWMAN GILFILLAN (March 2009)

Eugene Honey, *South Africa*, in GETTING THE DEAL THROUGH: FRANCHISE (2013) 172-178 (Philip F. Zeidman ed. 2013)

Taswell Papier, *Franchising in South Africa*, in FRANCHISING IN AFRICA: LEGAL AND BUSINESS CONSIDERATIONS 199-224 (Kendal H. Tyre, Jr. & Diana Vilmenay-Hammond eds. 2012)

Kendal H. Tyre, Jr., *A New Legal Landscape for Franchising in South Africa*, NIXON PEABODY LLP: FRANCHISING BUSINESS & LAW ALERT (September 2009)

## K.  Tunisia

Yessine Ferah, *Franchising in Tunisia*, in FRANCHISING IN AFRICA: LEGAL AND BUSINESS CONSIDERATIONS 225-245 (Kendal H. Tyre, Jr. & Diana Vilmenay-Hammond eds. 2012)

Kendal H. Tyre, Jr., Diana Vilmenay-Hammond, and Yessine Ferah, *New Franchise Legislation in Tunisia*, NIXON PEABODY LLP: FRANCHISE LAW ALERT (September 2010)

## L.  Zambia

Mabvuto Sakala, *Franchising in Zambia*, in FRANCHISING IN AFRICA: LEGAL AND BUSINESS CONSIDERATIONS 247-255 (Kendal H. Tyre, Jr. & Diana Vilmenay-Hammond eds. 2012)

www.ingramcontent.com/pod-product-compliance
Lightning Source LLC
Chambersburg PA
CBHW060325220326
41598CB00027B/4425